D1783742

MY DOG HATES MY DATE!

MY DOG HATES MY DATE!

HOW TO TEACH DOGS TO ACCEPT BABIES, TODDLERS & LOVERS

BY

AMY SHOJAI, CABC

A QUICK TIPS GUIDE, VOL. 1

Furry Muse Publications
Sherman TX 75091-1904

PUBLISHER'S NOTE

Publisher: Furry Muse Publishing
                PO Box 1904
                Sherman TX 75091-1904

TABLE OF CONTENTS

Dear Dog Lover,

Dear Dog Lover,

After writing 30+ pet behavior, vet care and training books, preserving "the bond" remains paws-down the most important goal of my career. That's the focus of my suspense fiction series, too, which includes an animal behaviorist, a trained Maine Coon cat, and a German Shepherd service dog viewpoint character. You can find my books listed here.

Preserving the pet-owner bond is why I wrote this quick-tips guide. The dog behavior advice is easy to do, and will help your "pet love" grow as your family grows.

You can find lots more free dog-centric advice by subscribing to my Bling, Bitches & Blood Blog at http://amyshojai.com. You can also subscribe to the free Pet Peeves newsletter and my ASK AMY YouTube. Stay tuned for some upcoming canine care and behavior webinars!

I love hearing what kind of furry info-tainment readers love best—yes, I do answer email! Please write me at amy@shojai.com. Or find me on Twitter (@amyshojai) as well as on Facebook.

Purrs,

MINE–MINE–MINE!

WHY SOME DOGS HATE NEW PEOPLE

In the perfect romantic fantasy, Charming-Fella and Slender-Ella meet, fall in love, and their pets Prince and Cinders welcome the relationship with howls of delight. When love is in the air, everyone's happy, right?

So why did Prince pee on *his* briefcase and chew the stiletto heels off *her* designer shoes? What's up when Cinders knocks down the kids and growls at the new baby? Why can't your pets love new human family members as much as you do?

Any change of routine can threaten a pets' sense of security. When you spend time with your new love, your pet misses you and feels lonely—and you SMELL weird, like that stranger! Dogs often feel proprietary toward their special human and take offense at new people invading their territory and taking the attention off of where it rightfully belongs; on the dog.

If you want to turn suspicion to adoration, don't forget to romance the pets too. Here's how to convince your dog to welcome him—or her—into the family.

Boost Pet Confidence. Some dogs feel shy or even fearful around strangers. Ask your human guest to avoid making eye contact, which can be threatening, and instead ignore the pet. That can generate curiosity and build confidence so shy dogs want to investigate further.

Let Pets Make the First Move. Don't force introductions. When the dog does approach, demonstrate how to greet your pet. Offer a closed hand below the pet's chin level for a proper dog sniff. Pets feel intimidated by strange hands coming down toward their heads, so avoid petting unless the dog asks for it.

Diffuse The Angst. Fearful dogs may benefit from using a canine pheromone product, an analogue of what mom-dogs produce when they nurse puppies. It works with adult dogs, too, to tell them, "Have no fear! Mom is here!" One of the most popular is called Comfort Zone with DAP and pheromone products are available from pet products stores as a spray or plug-in diffuser. The veterinary version of DAP is called Adaptil.

Love Pets With Goodies. Help your pets associate the new person in your life with only good things. For instance, ask your soul mate to fill the dog's food bowl, offer tasty treats, and engage in fun interactive games. Once your new love wins over the affection of one of the furry crew, that pet can be the role model for shyer dogs.

Don't Ignore The Fur-Kids. Make special time for your pets when you pay attention to the newcomer in the house. Ignoring the pack in favor of the new person tells your dogs they must compete for your attention. While you snuggle with your beau, toss tasty treats for dogs to fetch, so they associate the new person with good things. If they only get these "special" bonuses when your soul mate is present, dogs will be more likely to open their hearts to his or her presence.

But when love potions, animal magnetism and charm fail to win over reluctant pets—or your new human "soul mate" refuses to make the effort—consider this:

Maybe you should listen to what the pets are trying to tell you!

7 WAYS DOGS SHOW LOVE

There's no doubt we love our pets—but do our dogs love us back? Doggy shows of affection aren't always what humans expect. In fact, a pet's loving expressions might instead puzzle, aggravate or even offend some people. Here are 7 common ways your dog shows undying devotion.

1. **Dog howls** can mean your dog is lonely. Try scheduling extra face time with your special dog, or offer puzzle toys filled with treats to show your love. It's harder to howl when chewing something yummy.
2. **Dogs lean** against us. Yes, it can be pushy or awkward especially with big dogs, but it's a way of showing and asking for love and attention. Either sit down so he can lean and love, or teach him to "sit" before you dole out the attention.
3. **Dogs jump up**, not to knock you down, but to give a big kiss. A dog kiss isn't exactly the same as human kisses. Puppies lick the mom-dog's eyes and face to show deference. Adults give doggy kisses to humans they love and respect and aim at the face. Kneel to let him kiss you (if doggy smooches don't bother you). Or offer your hand for a sniff-and-smooch instead.

4. **Puppies pee and roll on their back** when owners come home—another way to show deference and declare their love and respect. Most pups outgrow the pee-party, but not the rolling over. Baring his tummy invites a friendly rub, so answer his request to show you love him, too.
5. **Dogs chew** to relieve stress and calm upset feelings, and also seek out owner-scented items like shoes or that Gucci handbag. Why not offer him a legal chew toy—stick it inside your shoe overnight so it has the appropriate "cologne" to really show your love!
6. **Dog crotch sniffs** may not seem all that loving but are the equivalent of a human hand shake. Request a "sit" instead, then pay him with attention.
7. **Doggy wags** that are low, loose and wide are technically a "distance-decreasing signal" that invites attention and love. Tail-less dogs wag their whole body.

We can't know for sure what they think, and every pet is different. Some dogs become very creative and keep us guessing! But there's no doubt pets love us back. The best gift we can give them is learning to understand them, foibles and all.

GREEN EYED MONSTERS?

5 TIPS TO JINX JEALOUS BEHAVIOR

Multiple dog households often arise from combining your pack with a new spouse's dogs, and many owners have experienced how quickly these dogs get their noses out of joint when a new family member (human or canine) enters the picture. Dogs truly believe you belong to them and may not want to share. The more dogs you have, the greater the chance that at least one of them will turn into a green-eyed monster over a new boyfriend, puppy, or human infant.

It is the people they love that will be most desired and guarded. Jealous dogs can act depressed and mope around the house, or become more rambunctious or destructive to get attention. Moderate jealousy usually goes away once Rex adjusts to the new person or pet, but serious cases can escalate to aggression to keep that "interloper" in the proper place. Proper introductions go a long way toward keeping the peace between dogs. Use these tips to avoid people jealousy.

Status Quo Routines. Jealousy is about fear of losing the one you love. When you have a new family member, don't exclude your resident dogs. Try to maintain the old, familiar schedule, and if you must change the routine, do so gradually several weeks before the newcomer arrives. Get the dog acclimated to the new schedule BEFORE you bring home someone new.

15

Go Neutral. Dogs feel proprietary about their house and yard, as well as you. Introduce your dogs to your new "beau" on neutral territory, at a dog park—in the same way you'd introduce Rex to a new canine friend, one dog at a time. Give your human love a chance to play ball and make friends with Rex before entering your house and becoming a threat.

Give 'Em More. Banishing the dogs from the room when your new love arrives makes your pets even more determined to compete for attention. Instead, try giving the dogs even MORE attention when s/he is there, and less when you're alone with the dogs.

Play Doggy Games. Play therapy is a powerful bonding tool between people and dogs. A game of Frisbee fetch or tug-the-toy can show your jealous dog the "new person" offers fun benefits for him. Reserve these favorite games to be played only with the new person.

Feed For Trust. Ask your fiancé to feed the dogs and play special fun games. The one who controls the resources (food and fun) is most respected in dog society. You want jealous dogs to associate the new person in your life with only good things, and be the key to tasty treats and Frisbee fun. Once your fiancé wins over one member of the pack, the others often see the light and start competing for equal time and attention.

HEALTH BENEFITS OF PETS

We live with pets because we make each other happy, but did you know there are health benefits to keeping cats and dogs? Multiple studies prove what puppy lovers already know—they're good for us! And they're especially good for babies and kids.

Dogs Reduce Stress

Dogs can be even more beneficial during times of stress. People with pets get sick less often, and recover more quickly than those without animal friends.

Your dog may lower blood pressure more effectively than medication. That's because the act of speaking dramatically increases blood pressure, and drugs don't block this effect. The only thing that counters elevated blood pressure that results from talking is focusing on something outside yourself—like a pet.

Your puppy doesn't even have to be present for this "pet effect" to work. It's simply enough to know he's waiting at home. Petting and stroking any friendly dog or cat also lowers blood pressure, so if you're pet-less, you could volunteer at the shelter or get your fur-fix at a neighbor's home. Petting is especially effective, though, when it's your own animals.

Pets Improve Childhood Development

The next time someone argues you should get rid of your pets before the new baby arrives, let 'em have it...in a kind and calm way, of course! Here's what they need to know.

There have been studies by Aline and Robert Kidd that show youngsters from pet-loving families score higher in cognitive, social, and motor development. Another researcher, Robert Poretsky, developed the Companion Animal Bonding Scale. The higher preschool children scored on this measurement tool, the higher their scores also were in all measures of development and empathy.

Don't worry about "dog germs," either. Infants and children who grow up with dogs and cats are less likely to develop allergies as they mature. And just as we want to provide proper socialization for kittens and puppies to accept—and even love—our babies and kids, it works both ways. Children properly introduced to cats and dogs during these early impressionable years will be more likely to enjoy loving relationships with pets the rest of their lives. I call it "activating the pet-love gene."

Pets Reduce Doctor Visits

According to a Japanese study, pet owners made 30 percent fewer visits to doctors than those who had no pet. Another survey by British researcher Dr. James Serpell showed that only one month after getting a dog or a cat, senior citizens had 50 percent fewer minor medical problems such as painful joints, hay fever, insomnia, constipation, anxiety, indigestion, colds and flu, general tiredness, palpitations or breathlessness, back pain, and headaches.

People who have suffered a heart attack—and own pets—recover more quickly and survive longer than heart attack survivors without pets. And those of us who live with a beloved dog or other pet experience only half as much blood pressure increase when stressed, as those without a pet.

Pets Increase Exercise

Keeping up with the dog can be a challenge. Chasing him around the house and yard, though, has other benefits.

Part of the pet effect has to do with increased exercise. I know that my exercise increased when Magical-Dawg came to live with us. He demands a game of fetch outside in the yard several times each day, and that gets me up and moving. Dogs won't take "no" for an answer, or let you sleep late if the food bowl is empty, and you can't ignore the puppy's potty needs the way you can a membership at the gym.

Exercise relieves anxiety, boredom, and depression. While others may look askance at goofy-acting humans, it's "legal" to play and have fun with your pets—which is as good for our own mental health as it is for the pets.

Pets keep us connected socially, too. Walking the dog at the neighborhood park or talking about your puppy at the pet food aisle at the grocery encourages contact that keeps us interested in life and other people.

Pets Relieve Pain and Anxiety

I'm not making this stuff up. Positron emission tomography (PET scan) is an imaging test that helps physicians to detect biochemical changes used to diagnose and monitor various health conditions. These tests show that touching a pet shuts down the pain-processing centers of the brain. Petting your dog relieves your own pain and also buffers anxiety, all without the side effects of Valium. In other words, a puppy on your lap can ease the pain in your ass-ets.

We often refer to "the bond" when talking about the love we feel for our pets. Science can actually measure this pet effect because thought and attitudes are influenced by changes in brain chemicals. These chemicals prompt feelings of elation, safety, tranquility, happiness, satisfaction, even love. Blood tests that measure these chemicals reveal that the levels increase for people—AND for the pets—when bonding takes place. In other words, when you bond with your dog, those feel-good chemicals and bonding happen for both you and the pet. There's no doubt about it, your dog returns your love!

Of course, if your puppy is a juvenile delinquent pooch that needs more training, he may raise your blood pressure by chewing illegal targets or having potty accidents. But all the aggravation is worth it.

Never discount how this pet effect impacts you and your dog. Consider dogs and cats to be a furry prescription that costs only a few pets and treats, and you'll both qualify for the health benefits.

DOG-TO-BABY INTRODUCTIONS

Dogs and babies can become great friends. But clueless pets—and active infants—also have the potential to terrorize or hurt one another. When you expect a new baby (or grandchild or visiting infant), prepare the dogs in advance to make sure interactions stay happy and safe.

Most dogs are curious about infants because they have so many interesting smells—milk, baby food, poop, what's not to love? Confident dogs often are very tolerant of babies, but toddlers can prove scary if they chase, pull tails, and make weird high-pitched noises. Don't expect every dog to feel the same about your kiddos. Some may love playing "pony" with a visiting toddler but a clueless young child could seriously injure your dog without meaning to.

Remember that compared to adult humans, babies and toddlers are Martians and particularly daunting because they don't yet understand and take direction as well as older children. Kids smell different than adults, have high-pitched funny voices, move in unpredictable ways, and appear threatening. Babies that crawl may mimic prey behavior in their sounds and actions. Wary dogs may switch into play-aggression or become defensive and try to drive away the scary creature. Neither option is good.

8 WAYS TO PREPARE BEFORE BABY COMES HOME

You've got nine months before the infant comes home. Prepare ahead of time so the new routine, furniture and even some of the smells are familiar to your dogs by the time the baby arrives.

1. **Let Them Explore.** Allow your pets to investigate the redecorated nursery so they won't feel left out. This is especially true if they previously had free access to the room—banning them may cause behavior issues when they're left out. Think about dog-proofing the room so baby toys and diaper pail are out of dog-munching range.
2. **Manage Access.** Install a baby gate in the doorway so your dogs can see into the room and be a part of the joy but are kept out when you can't supervise their action.
3. **Practice Crying.** Fussy babies sound similar to prey so it can be upsetting for some dogs to hear this. Record infant cries and play back to your pets to acclimate them to the sounds. Your dogs may ignore the sound or act curious, and reward either behavior with calm praise.

4. **Offer Positive Associations.** Give the dog special treats when they act in a calm way near the baby's areas.
5. **Dab On Baby Smells.** Begin wearing baby powder or lotion weeks in advance so your dog associates the aromas with a beloved and safe human they already know.
6. **Adjust Your Schedule.** A new baby throws your old routine out the window. Prepare the dogs so they already understand the new timeline, and be sure to include special DOG TIME so they don't feel totally neglected. While you're understandably happy, excited (and exhausted!) with a new baby in the house, excluding your dogs from your joy only confuses them at best.
7. **Give Dogs An Advance Sniff.** When the baby finally arrives, bring home something scented with the infant so that your dog has an advance introduction. For instance, bring home a tee shirt or baby blanket the baby has already worn.
8. **"Sock" Your Dogs.** No, I don't mean to hit them—but for nervous dogs who might act fearful, use a bit of the Comfort Zone with DAP or another calming product, and spritz on baby socks. That way the footwear contains the canine "no fear" pheromones that keep dogs calm. Then have the baby wear the socks, and voila! Your baby now smells like something safe so your dog more readily recognizes the infant as safe and an acceptable member of the household.

4 TIPS WHEN BABY COMES HOME

When you bring home the baby, treat the event in a matter-of-fact manner, and don't make a big deal of the introduction (even though it's momentous, of course!). You want the dog to understand this is a normal, expected part of his life.

Act Normal. Don't force the introduction. But if the dogs act interested, allow them to sniff the baby's foot, perhaps (with that scented sock). If the dogs are too excited, do this one dog at a time so you aren't overwhelmed. By allowing your dog to actually look at, smell, and touch that creature that's so very different, he'll understand there's nothing to fear.

Give Ownership. Try referring to the child as "Rex's baby." Yes, it sounds silly, but just saying the words changes your attitude which can be comforting and calming to your dog.

Reward Calm Confidence. Praise the dogs when they act well, and ignore shy or fearful behavior.

Associate Good Things. Pets quickly learn to associate the baby with what's important to them—if they get ignored or yelled at when the infant is near, the baby will acquire negative associations. Figure out what your dog loves and link it to the baby's presence. Maybe you can toss treats when the baby naps on your lap, for instance.

6 TIPS FOR SUCCESSFUL

DOG-TO-TODDLER/KID INTROS

Once babies start walking they can become more interesting—and challenging—for your dogs. Many of the same dog-to-baby introductions apply, but in addition, refer to these tips for toddlers and older children.

- **Provide A Safe Retreat.** Be sure your dogs have a canine sanctuary that's off limits to kids. Even pets that adore children need private time and a place to go where they know they won't be pestered.
- **Teach Kids Limits.** Ask toddlers to practice petting a stuffed toy or the child's own arm or head. Young kids take time to learn that dogs aren't stuffed animals, and can be hurt and lash out from pulled tails or ears.
- **DON'T Hug!** For people, hugging means affection and love. But in dog language, a hug can be a threat or challenge, and dogs may respond with defensive growls (or worse!). Yes, some dogs can be taught to tolerate hugs but for safety's sake, avoid encouraging children (or anyone) to hug dogs—especially unknown pooches.

- **Practice Puppy Quiet-Talk**. High pitched screams could potentially prompt the dogs to aggress toward each other or the child. Challenge children to talk in an inside "puppy-talk" voice that entices dogs to come near for pets. You can explain that just like children can get frightened of scary sounds, dogs can be scared and it takes very talented kids to know how to be pooch-friendly.
- **Ignore The Dogs.** Staring is a challenge that can stress some dogs, especially stares from kids that are eye-to-eye level. But when ignored, dogs may be intrigued enough to investigate on their own. So challenge your toddler or older child to an "ignore the pup" game, and see how long they can pretend the dog isn't there. In most cases, a confident canine will eventually approach.
- **Seat The Kids.** Dogs take turns playing chase-and-tackle games, so when chased by toddlers they may get too rough without meaning to. Make it a dog rule that young kids must sit before they can pet the dog, and that the dog gets to approach. Forcing a dog to sit still for a child's attention may cause your pet to avoid the child in future—instead make it the dog's choice and a fun, rewarding experience. Once seated, the child can lure and entice the dogs' interest and interaction with a toy. Playing builds a positive relationship that can grow into love.

- **Offer Treats.** When dogs still act reluctant to approach, find a smelly, tasty treat the pet loves but ONLY gets from the child. While sitting on the floor, the child should gently toss the treat to (not AT) the dog. That prevents accidental nips from overly enthusiastic pooches eager to snarf up the treat.

WANT TO PLEASE YOUR LOVER? PAMPER THE POOCH!

Americans consider our pets to be best friends, soul mates, family members, and even surrogate children. But pet lovers around the world also adore their pets, and some folks wish their significant other would just act a bit more like their dog--and I don't mean stealing your TV remote, either.

One-fifth of adults would prefer to be with their pet, according to a joint global poll by Reuters/Ipsos. The survey of 24,000 people in 23 countries found 21 percent of adults would rather spend Valentine's Day with their pet than their spouse.

Get a load of these stats: nearly half (49 percent) of those surveyed in Turkey were most likely to want to spend that special day with their pet over their partner. Other nations where pets often prevail over people are India (41 percent), Japan (30 percent), China (29 percent), the US (27 percent) and Australia (25 percent).

One-quarter of people under age 35 were more likely to choose their pets, versus 18 percent of those aged 35 to 54, and 14 percent of people aged over 55. Men and women, however, were equally split.

Want Love? Be Like Your Dog

Surveys by the American Kennel Club found even more startling results and reported that nearly 90 percent of women wish their boyfriend or husband was more like their dog. The survey revealed that 65 percent of respondents would pick their dog to be their Valentine over a human companion!

The top canine quality people wished their human Valentines had is that they're always happy to see them (40 percent). Following not far behind is "willing to go anywhere with you" at 25 percent, "loves snuggling" at 15 percent, and "doesn't talk back" at 12 percent.

Canine qualities women look for in men include a perennial good mood, willingness to spend time together, eagerness to cuddle on the couch, and being happy to eat her cooking without complaint. The survey also indicated women appreciated how dogs helped motivate them to exercise.

Canine qualities that men appreciate in women include being as happy to spend time at home as out on the town, offering enthusiastic greetings when he returns home, and not getting mad when he wants to watch sports. Men also liked it that dogs were "up" for anything he wants to do. Men also wish their significant other shared some of the same qualities as their dog, especially the quality of "always being in a good mood."

Babe Magnet?

The poll also revealed that 58 percent of men consider a puppy to be a foolproof "babe magnet" in the park. In fact, 46 percent of women polled admitted they'd stop and talk to anyone with a cute puppy. You'd better like your date's dog, too, or be a darn good actor. A whopping 66 percent of owners said they wouldn't even consider dating someone who didn't like their pet.

Listen To Fido

Based on these results, men and women should go to the dog for hints on pleasing the special humans in their lives. In fact, people have such strong bonds with their canine companions that their human soul mates may become jealous. Reasons include dedicating "too much" time to the pet, preferring to cuddle with the dog rather than their mate, or that the dog "likes me better."

And if love goes away, be prepared for a canine custody battle. Sixty percent of dog owners said if they split up with their significant other, they'd definitely get the dog. Married dog owners were more than twice as likely as their single counterparts to say they'd have to call in Judge Judy to settle ownership.

So listen to your dog to help you choose the ideal human love connection. Otherwise, you risk being dogged by the consequences.

BREAKING UP?

WHEN DOGS MOURN THE MISSING

Dogs get depressed for the same reasons we do. Changes in relationships can be an emotional time for the humans involved. You may be depressed, angry, relieved, sad, or all of the above when your romance ends, but at least you know what happened.

Your dog may have learned to love your partner—after all, you've used all the tips in this book, right? And when it ends, pets won't understand why a human friend moves out and disappears. Just as a new baby or new spouse can leave dogs feeling blue when they're no longer the center of your world, once that attachment develops, your pet can mourn the loss when the relationship ends.

Depressed dogs may sleep more than usual. They either want to eat all the time, become finicky, or refuse to eat altogether. Depressed pets often act lethargic, and many retreat from the world by hiding in the basement. These feelings are as natural for dogs as they are for owners, but they can cause health problems or upset feelings in the rest of the pack if they go on too long. Dogs must work through the grieving process but a number of things can help.

Talk to your dog. Losing a loved one makes you depressed, too, and the pack's grief can reflect your own. They won't always comprehend all the words, but understand your intent. Be positive around mourning dogs and when you can't, simply say, "I'm sad, but it's not your fault." They'll understand and it will help.

Give him a massage. Give Rex special attention such as alone time with you, or a petting massage. Petting your dog and his touch in return can help you both reduce stress from the situation.

Keep it upbeat. Avoid too much babying, though, or your natural urge to pamper rewards and encourages the behaviors to continue or even become worse. Give Rex attention but in an upbeat, enthusiastic manner. That can help you feel better, too. Dogs tend to reflect the emotions of their human loved ones, so acting happy helps your dog get through the angst, too.

Send messages. When a human family member leaves only temporarily, perhaps for a work trip, vacation or college, keeping scented items as reminders can help soothe pets until the beloved's return. Seal a few unwashed socks in a baggy, and bring one out now and then for your dog to sleep or play with as a security blanket. The long-distance human can also mail scented objects home to the dog, or call and speak to him on the phone. For dogs that get more wound up (and you know the person won't be returning), avoid the phone calls or scented reminders as that can prolong the healing process.

Take a break. A weekend away to a new place can help some dogs make the transition to a new life without the missing friend.

Shine a light. Offer your pet a sunbath on the back porch every day for twenty minutes or so. Light therapy has been shown to be beneficial to people suffering from depression, because it affects the production of hormones from the pituitary and endocrine glands and also helps raise canine spirits.

Offer some harmony. Music affects emotions in pets just like people. Slow soft music soothes upset feelings of the mourning dogs, while peppy music with a driving rhythm can energize them, because our heart rate and brain waves tend to mimic (entrain) these patterns. Music that reminds your pet of happier times—perhaps associated with a loved one who has gone away—can free up the emotional responses in your pets so they can heal and come out of the depression. Harp music works especially well.

Play games. Counteract depression with games or "canine work" to do so the dogs must think about something else.

Get an Rx. In severe cases, your veterinarian can prescribe antidepressant drugs to help a severely depressed dog through the process. The herb St. John's Wort, a natural antidepressant that can take the edge off your pet's grief, should only be given for a very short time. The dosage depends on the individual dog.

THANK YOU FOR READING!

Dear Reader,

I began writing about pets more than twenty years ago—in dog years I should be dead! I hope you enjoyed reading **MY DOG HATES MY DATE**! and that it's made a love connection between your human loves and furry family members.

For dog-to-dog angst and a whole lot more canine behavior tips and tricks, find detailed how-to answers in the full-length book, **COMPETABILITY: SOLVING BEHAVIOR PROBLEMS IN YOUR MULTI-DOG HOUSEHOLD.**

Many times I hear from readers who share stories about their dogs and cats, and I'd love to hear from you. Maybe YOUR pet's heartwarming story could be published on my blog at AmyShojai.com or even included in a future book. All dogs deserve to be famous!

I'd like to ask a big favor—could you please post a review of this book (loved it, hated it) as I'd enjoy your feedback. You may not realize how much influence readers like you have to make or break a book simply by sharing your thoughts in a review. So if you have the time, please share your thoughts.

Thank you so much for spending your time with me. Now…go pet your pets!

Woofs & doggy grins,

Amy Shojai

BIO: Amy Shojai, CABC is an IAABC certified animal behavior consultant and a nationally known authority on pet care. She is the award-winning author of more than two-dozen dog and cat books and thousands of articles and columns. She served as the Puppies Expert at Puppies.About.com, and the behavior expert at Cats.About.com, and regularly appears on national radio and television including Animal Planet DOGS 101 and CATS 101.

Amy addresses a wide range of fun-to-serious issues in her work, covering training, behavior, health care, and medical topics. She also writes the September Day "Thrillers With Bite" series featuring a German Shepherd service dog viewpoint character.

She and her husband live with Magic the German Shepherd, a seventeen-year-old Siamese "wannabe" Seren, and an adolescent kitten Karma (the dog's best friend). Amy can be reached at her website at shojai.com where you can subscribe to her PET PEEVES Newsletter, like her on Facebook.com/amyshojai.cabc, follow on Twitter @amyshojai, and check out her Bling, Bitches & Blood Blog at AmyShojai.com.

Lightning Source UK Ltd.
Milton Keynes UK
UKHW020644160822
407375UK00009B/675

9 781948 366540